D1524592

BE YOUR OWN BOSS

PLAN A RECYCLING BUSINESS

STEPHANE HILLARD

PowerKiDS press
New York

Published in 2021 by The Rosen Publishing Group, Inc.
29 East 21st Street, New York, NY 10010

Portions of this work were originally authored by Emma Carlson Berne and published as *Run Your Own Recycling Business*. All new material in this edition authored by Stephane Hillard.

Editor: Elizabeth Krajnik
Book Design: Reann Nye

Photo Credits: Cover Dave & Les Jacobs/DigitalVision/Getty Images; series art stas11/Shutterstock.com; p. 5 Eugene Gologursky/Getty Images Entertainment/Getty Images; p. 7 Dmytro Zinkevych/Shutterstock.com; pp. 9, 17 Rawpixel.com/Shutterstock.com; p. 11 Jose Luis Pelaez Inc/DigitalVision/Getty Images; p. 13 Mr.anaked /Shutterstock.com; p. 15 Image Source/Image Source/Getty Images; p. 19 Jorgefontestad/iStock / Getty Images Plus/Getty Images; p. 21 Dev Carr/Cultura/Getty Images; p. 22 Hurst Photo/Shutterstock.com.

Library of Congress Cataloging-in-Publication Data

Names: Hillard, Stephane, author.
Title: Plan a recycling business / Stephane Hillard.
Description: New York : PowerKids Press, 2021. | Series: Be your own boss |
    Includes index.
Identifiers: LCCN 2020003205 | ISBN 9781725319011 (paperback) | ISBN
    9781725319035 (library binding) | ISBN 9781725319028 (6 pack)
Subjects: LCSH: Recycling industry–Juvenile literature. | Money-making
    projects for children–Juvenile literature.
Classification: LCC HD9975.A2 .H545 2021 | DDC 628.4/4580681–dc23
LC record available at https://lccn.loc.gov/2020003205

Manufactured in the United States of America

Some of the images in this book illustrate individuals who are models. The depictions do not imply actual situations or events.

CPSIA Compliance Information: Batch #CSPK20. For Further Information contact Rosen Publishing, New York, New York at 1-800-237-9932.

Find us on

CONTENTS

YOUNG ENTREPRENEURS

Have you ever wanted to buy a new video game but didn't have enough money? Do you want to save money for college? Some people save up the money they get from their parents. However, others choose to start their own business. These people are young entrepreneurs. An entrepreneur is a person who starts a business and is willing to possibly lose money in order to make money.

This book will show you the steps to follow to plan and start your own business, including making a business plan, creating a **budget**, advertising, and more. In time, you'll be able to enjoy your business's **profits**.

Not all entrepreneurs are adults. When she was just four years old, Mikaila Ulmer began making and selling lemonade. Today, Me & the Bees lemonade is sold in many stores, including Whole Foods Market.

SUPPLY AND DEMAND

The first step when starting a business is deciding what kind of business you're going to start. Every business should provide people with a product or service. Your business should supply, or fulfill, a demand, or need, in your community.

Before you can start your business, make a list of products or services you think you could provide. Then do some **research**. You can avoid **competition** by choosing a product or service that isn't already being provided.

Starting a recycling business is great for young entrepreneurs. You can collect the bottles, cans, and paper people throw out and return them to a recycling center for money.

Recycling is good for the Earth too, since the recyclables won't end up in a **landfill**.

CREATING A BUSINESS PLAN

Before you start your recycling business, you'll need to create a business plan. This plan outlines where, when, why, and how you'll run your business. First, you should decide which recyclable items you'd like to collect.

Then, you should decide where you'll collect your items. Will you collect recyclables from houses in your neighborhood? If so, you'll need to find a way to **transport** the items, such as a wagon or wheelbarrow. Will you have people drop off cans and bottles at your house?

Next, decide when you'll collect your items. Will you collect recyclables on a certain day?

GOOD BUSINESS

The type of recyclables you'd like to collect will help you figure out what supplies you'll need. Make a list of these supplies. This will help you make your budget later.

Some recycling centers only accept glass and plastic. You may have to take paper and aluminum recyclables to a different recycling center.

BUDGETING AND EXPENSES

Your recycling business, like all other businesses, will have expenses. Expenses are costs that arise throughout the course of doing business. Creating a budget for your recycling business will allow you to keep track of your expenses.

To create your budget, make a list of everything you'll need to start and run your business. Check how much money you have saved. Do you have enough saved to run your business for the first month? If not, you'll need to borrow some money, most likely from your parents. Then you'll need to make a plan to repay them.

GOOD BUSINESS

If recycling centers allow you to return items for cash, figure out how much they'll give you per item. This will help you **estimate** your profits!

Creating a budget helps you keep track of your expenses and earnings. However, it can also help you make a savings plan for things you'll need to purchase later on.

THE IMPORTANCE OF ADVERTISING

Advertising is how you'll let people know you're starting a recycling business. You can advertise by telling people in your neighborhood, which is called word of mouth, by making flyers or signs, or by putting an ad in your local newspaper.

On your advertising **materials** you should put where and when you'll collect recyclables. You can highlight the fact that you'll be sorting and hauling the recyclables to the recycling center. Advertising should convince people to use your recycling service instead of taking their recyclables to a recycling center themselves or using another recycling service.

GOOD BUSINESS

Why did you start your recycling business? Are you saving money for college? Are you trying to keep the Earth clean? Tell possible customers your reasons to make them want to use your service.

Even if city workers collect recyclables, they may not always make it to the recycling center. They may end up in a forest or in a body of water.

HIRING EMPLOYEES

Hiring **employees** will make running your recycling business easier. You'll also be able to collect more recyclables and, as a result, make more of a profit. You'll need to figure out how your employees can be the most useful.

You'll have to pay your employees. If you pay them an hourly wage, it'll be easier to know how much business you'll have to do. If you pay them a percentage of the profits, it may be harder to know how much business you'll have to do. However, your employees might work harder if they know they'll get paid more.

You can hire your friends or siblings as employees. Make sure they sign a **contract**, which states how much and how often they'll be paid and what they'll be required to do.

You can also hire your parents or other trusted adults as employees. They can drive you and your recyclables to the recycling center. You'll need to pay them as well. How much you pay them should cover the money they spend on gas. It should also cover part of the wear and tear on their car.

Don't forget, this person will spend time they might otherwise spend doing something else to help you run your business. You should also pay them for their time. Will you pay them up front for their help or will you pay them after?

If someone drives you around your neighborhood to collect recyclables, make sure you pay them for this too.

GATHERING SUPPLIES

A few days before the first time you collect recyclables, you'll need to figure out what supplies you'll need. Look at the list you made earlier. Do you already own some of these things? What will you need to buy?

You'll probably need large garbage bags to hold the bottles and cans, twist ties to secure the tops of the garbage bags, a pair of protective gloves, supplies for your advertising materials, and, most importantly, some way to transport your recyclables, such as a wagon. You may also need a place to store the recyclables.

Depending on how many recyclables you collect and when you can drop them off at the recycling center, you may need to store the recyclables in large containers.

TIME TO RECYCLE!

Now that you've created your business plan, made a budget, advertised, hired employees, and gathered your supplies, you're ready for business.

Carry a notebook with you. In the notebook, keep track of your collecting appointments. If you miss an appointment, that customer may not want to use your recycling services anymore. They may also tell their friends not to use your services.

Also keep track of the money you make and spend in your notebook. This is where you'll write down how much money you make at the recycling center and how much you have to pay your employees.

GOOD BUSINESS

Make sure you're keeping your budget in mind. If you're spending more money than you're taking in, you'll need to find a way to fix that. Consider collecting more recyclables or working longer hours.

If your customers are happy with your recycling services, ask them to write you a **review** and tell their friends. The more customers you have, the bigger your business can become.

BUSINESS CHECKLIST

- Address a community need
- Create a business plan
- Find a local recycling center, ask what items they take, ask how much they pay
- Create a budget
- Purchase supplies for your business and for advertising materials
- Advertise your recycling services
- Hire employees
- Collect recyclables
- Take recyclables to recycling center
- Enjoy the profits

GLOSSARY

budget: A plan used to decide the amount of money that can be spent and how it will be spent.

competition: A person or group you're trying to succeed against.

contract: A legal agreement between people, companies, etc.

employee: A person who is paid to work for another.

estimate: To give or form a general idea of something.

landfill: An area where waste is buried under the ground.

material: Matter from which something is made or can be made.

profit: The gain after all the expenses are subtracted from the total amount received.

research: Careful study that is done to find and report new knowledge about something.

review: A piece of writing about the quality of something, such as a book or a business.

transport: To carry from one place to another.

INDEX

WEBSITES

Due to the changing nature of Internet links, PowerKids Press has developed an online list of websites related to the subject of this book. This site is updated regularly. Please use this link to access the list:
www.powerkidslinks.com/byoboss/recycling

24